This book is dedicated to Lynne,
simply the smartest connection
I ever made

CONTENTS

THE POCKET GUIDE FOR
NERVOUS NETWORKERS

INTRODUCTION

"The richest
people
in the world
look for and
build networks,
everyone else
looks for work"

Robert Kiyosaki

THIS BOOK IS YOURS

If you are in business and know that networking is crucial to your success but are nervous about networking, this book is yours.

If you have done some networking already but know that you could improve, this book is yours.

If you know that networking is a great way to develop your personal brand but are nervous about getting going, this book is yours.

If your boss has told you to do more networking to bring in more clients, but you're not the sort of person that makes friends easily, this book is yours.

If you are nervous about approaching strangers and starting conversations, this book is yours.

If you would like to own the secrets of over two decades of successful business networking right NOW to keep in your pocket or bag, this book is yours.

If you want a handy source of tips that you can dip into whenever you need it, then without doubt...

... this book is yours

"The successful networkers I know, the ones receiving tons of referrals and feeling truly happy about themselves, continually put the other person's needs ahead of their own"

Bob Burg

ABOUT THIS BOOK

Networking is one of the key skills required for running a successful business. There are few other business activities more important than knowing how to make connections with people we value.

Humans involved in commerce have known this since the earliest days of bartering and merchant trading, and it is as true now as it ever was.

Yet where do we go to learn these skills? We are certainly not taught them at school. Business courses don't teach you how to start conversations with strangers and find something in common that may develop into ongoing business. That is where this book proves itself essential.

Keep it handy. Keep it in your pocket or bag and give it a quick glance before going into a networking event. Make notes in the pages which we have deliberately kept blank, so you can gradually customise this book with your own observations and reminders.

It's your book. Never lend it out. If you know someone who could benefit from it, get them their own copy to customise.

Now, start connecting…

"Becoming
well known
(at least among
your prospects
and connections)
is the
most valuable
element in the
connection
process"

Jeffrey Gitomer

ABOUT THE AUTHOR

Ash Mashhadi is the founder Partner of a successful web design and social media consultancy. He has been helping businesses to connect creatively with their clients for over two decades. He also acts as a business mentor for small businesses and start-ups.

People who know him often refer to Ash as 'The Inspiration Guy' because he loves to help businesses succeed and because of the way that conversations with him tend to end up being motivational.

Ash has appeared on national TV and BBC radio as a business expert. He is a lively and engaging speaker and has written for numerous publications both online and offline.

Ash has written this book to help small business owners and reluctant networkers realise their potential. You don't have to be outgoing, loud or brash to be a successful business networker. Use this book as a gentle guiding hand when you need some motivation, inspiration, or just a few ideas to help you develop your business success.

"You can make
more friends in
two months
by becoming
interested in
other people than
you can in
two years by
trying to get
other people
interested in you"

Dale Carnegie

LET'S CONNECT

The first step of all networking is about making a connection. The second step is to find a way to give value to that connection so that the other person wants to keep coming back to you. The third step comes when they recognise your value and want to reciprocate. That's how it works.

If you think that connecting with the author of this book, Ash Mashhadi, may add value to your business network, here's how to connect with him:

TWITTER

@inspirationguy

FACEBOOK

http://facebook.com/ashmashhadi

LINKEDIN

http://www.linkedin.com/in/ashmashhadi

THE POCKET GUIDE FOR
NERVOUS NETWORKERS

PREPARATION

NOTES

NETWORKING
STARTS
BEFORE
YOU
ENTER THE ROOM

Networking is a 24/7 activity now. Outside of any networking event, people are looking at one another's social media activity and measuring your value by who knows you. That's only scary if you've been neglecting your online and offline profile.

THE POCKET GUIDE FOR
NERVOUS NETWORKERS

NOTES

PREPARATION

PRACTISE

YOUR 30-SECOND PITCH
UNTIL IT SOUNDS AND FEELS

NATURAL

Tip: it's not the exact words, it's the meaning of the words.

NOTES

UNDERSTAND
YOUR

USP

Most people don't know their unique selling point, so knowing yours gives you an immediate advantage. What makes you uniquely valuable to others is your USP; the ability to communicate that unique quality sets you apart from your competitors.

NOTES

GET
A
NETWORKING
BUDDY

Find someone else who wants to improve
and work together. Practise pitching and
exchanging feedback until you feel like you
are professionals.

NOTES

Answer this Question:

WHAT
DO I
WANT
TO ACHIEVE BY
NETWORKING?

Use the Notes page opposite to record your answer. For example:

"Get to know some people who are interested in what I do", or

"Find out what people think of my new business idea or marketing idea"

Too many people start networking without setting a quantifiable goal.

NOTES

IS YOUR
ENERGY
LEVEL
HIGH
ENOUGH?

Boring people are generally ignored at
networking events. Raise your energy level
with some networking exercises (see the
following pages for some ideas and
generate your own too).

NOTES

Networking Exercise

PRACTISE
YOUR 30-SECOND PITCH
WITH YOUR
NETWORKING BUDDY

5 TIMES
(OR UNTIL IT FEELS NATURAL)

Ask your buddy to rate your performance
using a scale from 1-10 on mutually agreed
criteria that you want to work on improving.
For example: volume, body language,
shyness, clarity, focus.

NOTES

Networking Exercise

DELIVER YOUR
30-SECOND PITCH

BACKWARDS

3 TIMES

WITH YOUR
NETWORKING BUDDY

If you can't deliver your key messages backwards, as well as forwards, you don't really know them and will be likely to forget them at the event. Remember: it's not a script, it's a conversation, so don't just recite a script both ways, cover each point in forward and reverse order.

NOTES

Networking Exercise
HOLD A
CONVERSATION
WITH YOUR
NETWORKING BUDDY
FROM
OPPOSITE ENDS
OF A
LARGE ROOM

This will teach you to project your voice with clarity. An ideal skill in a crowded room. It will raise your energy levels, plus it's fun.

NOTES

JOIN
A
PUBLIC
SPEAKING
CLUB LIKE
TOASTMASTERS
INTERNATIONAL

This will improve your ability to pitch, your sense of timing, confidence, and general presentation skills. This is a 5 star tip, ignore it at your peril!

NOTES

GET A

LOT

BETTER

AT

PUBLIC
SPEAKING

Attending a few sessions at your public speaking club is not nearly enough. Constant improvement pays dividends. After presenting to a roomful of expectant faces, talking in a one-to-one networking situation will no longer seem nerve-wracking.

NOTES

PAY A
DESIGNER
(NOT A PRINTER)
TO DESIGN YOU A
BUSINESS CARD
THAT MAKES PEOPLE SAY
"WOW!"

Your job is to stand out from the crowd, not fit in. Make sure your business card does not end up in the bin the next day.

P.S. You're not a designer.

NOTES

REHEARSE
WHAT
TO SAY
IF YOU MET A
KEY
INFLUENCER

What do you want from making a connection? What value do you offer them? Know this before you meet. Preparation means you won't be tongue-tied when the opportunity comes up.

NOTES

BE SELECTIVE
ABOUT
WHERE
YOU NETWORK

Be discerning. Don't become known as the kind of person that would go to the opening of a paper bag. We've all met them. Some networking events are a waste of your time.

THE POCKET GUIDE FOR
NERVOUS NETWORKERS

NOTES

46

VISIT
MORE THAN
ONE
NETWORKING
CLUB
OR
EVENT
REGULARLY

Spread your net wide to avoid meeting the
same people everywhere.

NOTES

AVOID
CLUBS THAT
BAN YOU
FROM JOINING
OTHER
CLUBS

They exist. Really. Why restrict your circle of
influence? It's meant to be a club, not a cult.

NOTES

ATTRACTION

NOTES

ATTRACTION

BE
YOURSELF

Don't adopt a 'persona'. The authentic you
is more attractive than any identity you
could invent.

THE POCKET GUIDE FOR NERVOUS NETWORKERS

NOTES

WRITE A BOOK
ABOUT A TOPIC
THAT SHARES
YOUR
EXPERTISE

It is a great ice-breaker and you could even give a copy to potential clients. Much more memorable than a business card!

NOTES

BUILD

A

STRONG

PERSONAL

BRAND

An outstanding personal brand means
people seek you out. This is a hallmark of
people that offer exceptional value.

NOTES

IT'S NOT ABOUT
WHO YOU KNOW
IT'S ABOUT
WHO KNOWS

YOU

Your personal brand is what sets you apart from the crowd. A great brand reputation can open more doors for you than almost anything else.

NOTES

DEVELOP
A
REPUTATION
AS
SOMEONE
WORTH
KNOWING

This way, the right people will seek you out,
instead of you having to look for them.

NOTES

HELP
PEOPLE IN
YOUR NETWORK
MAKE
VALUABLE
CONNECTIONS

The value you bring to your network
determines the value of your network. When
you need anything, you'll have access to a
whole group of people willing to help you.

NOTES

FIRST:

BE GENUINELY

INTERESTED

IN

OTHER PEOPLE

SECOND:

LEARN TO

IDENTIFY

WHAT PEOPLE NEED

THIRD:

BECOME

A

CONNECTOR

NOTES

FOCUS ON
MEETING THE
RIGHT PEOPLE
NOT THE
MOST PEOPLE

Collecting business cards only fills your
drawer, not your wallet.

NOTES

WRITE
EXPERT
ARTICLES
FOR INDUSTRY
MAGAZINES
AND
WEBSITES

Don't expect to be paid for them unless
you're a professional writer; instead look for
the value you will get from sharing your
expertise.

NOTES

USE
SOCIAL
MEDIA
TO BUILD
YOUR
PERSONAL
BRAND

Social networking is simply the fastest way
to reach lots of people and businesses
interested in what you do.

NOTES

SOCIAL
NETWORKING

NOTES

GET SOME
TRAINING
ON USING
SOCIAL
NETWORKING
EFFECTIVELY

You'll stand out from everyone else who is just winging it, or from those using business social media like they do their personal social media.

Always be as professional as you would in real life. You never know who might be reading what you post.

NOTES

START

A

BLOG

Create a new blog post at least once a month. Write posts that share your expertise and ethos. Use social media to attract readers to your blog, vlog, or podcast.

NOTES

WRITE

AN

E-BOOK

Use it to build your mailing list by offering it as a reward for signing up. If you don't have a mailing list, start one. Also use it to build your online profile as an expert.

NOTES

MAKE AN
ACCOUNT ON
ONLY
THE MAIN
SOCIAL
MEDIA
PLATFORMS

You don't have time to be everywhere.
Share engaging content that's relevant and
valuable to your market. This will help build
your personal brand. Don't be afraid to
share your expertise.

NOTES

CONSIDER
JOINING
SOCIAL
PLATFORMS
WHILE THEY
ARE STILL
NEW

You need to be where your potential clients
are. Assess the potential appeal of new
platforms, but don't join everything or all
your time will disappear.

NOTES

GET
STRATEGIC
WITH YOUR
SOCIAL
MEDIA

Use it to bypass gatekeepers and get
directly in touch with boardroom-level
connections and potential clients.

Your social media can be a back-channel
direct to your next clients.

NOTES

SHARE LINKS
THAT ARE
RELEVANT
TO YOUR
EXPERTISE

Use it to enhance your personal brand and reputation. For example, you could share case studies, tips, or advice.

SOCIAL NETWORKING

THE POCKET GUIDE FOR NERVOUS NETWORKERS

NOTES

SOCIAL NETWORKING

HAVE A
PROFESSIONAL
PHOTOGRAPH
TAKEN FOR
YOUR PROFILE

Don't hide behind your logo, it's hard to
make friends with a graphic.

THE POCKET GUIDE FOR NERVOUS NETWORKERS

NOTES

SOCIAL NETWORKING

IDENTIFY
KEY
INFLUENCERS
IN YOUR FIELD AND
CONNECT
WITH THEM

Show that you're a person of value by
sharing quality information and comments,
and you'll attract connections to you.

THE POCKET GUIDE FOR NERVOUS NETWORKERS

NOTES

ADD
YOUR
SOCIAL MEDIA
DETAILS TO YOUR
BUSINESS CARD
AND
WEBSITE

You'll be surprised how many people forget
to take this basic step.

NOTES

SHARE
SOMETHING OF
VALUE
WITH YOUR
NETWORK
EVERY DAY

Never ever miss a single day. Becoming a consistent source of quality makes you a valuable resource. Others will soon start recommending you.

NOTES

SHARE

THE

BLOG POSTS

AND

MESSAGES

OF

INFLUENCERS

Real influencers always thank you.
Acknowledge their thanks. Ask a question.
After a while you'll find it easier to engage
them in conversation.

NOTES

WORK HARD
AND
IMPROVE
YOUR
WRITING

Great leaders are great communicators.
Offer to guest post on recognised industry
blogs. That will introduce you to much
bigger audiences. It may take a while but
you'll be accepted eventually… if you keep
working hard to improve your writing.

NOTES

ATTENDING
EVENTS

THE POCKET GUIDE FOR
NERVOUS NETWORKERS

NOTES

ARRIVE EARLY
AND
LEAVE LATE

This will mean that the lazy networkers won't be in your way and you can more easily approach key influencers. During peak times, at an event they're usually surrounded by people seeking their time and attention.

NOTES

WHEN YOU

MEET

SOMEONE

NEW

USE THEIR

NAME

It will fix it in your head and help them feel
more comfortable around you (provided you
don't creep them out by using it in every
sentence!).

NOTES

DON'T WAIT
TO BE
APPROACHED

ATTENDING EVENTS

If you're a new face, make the first move.
Proactive communicators are the ones we
remember. If you start the conversation first,
you've saved someone else the trouble of
doing it and they may have been dreading it.
Everyone gets nervous sometimes.

THE POCKET GUIDE FOR NERVOUS NETWORKERS

NOTES

MAKE THE OPENING

3 WORDS

OF YOUR PITCH

CREATIVE

… and make the last 3 words memorable. A big finish is remarkably powerful. This way, yours may be the only pitch they remember the next day. Remember too, that not every encounter is an invitation to pitch.

NOTES

YOUR
STRONGEST
NETWORKING
ASSET
IS YOUR
SMILE

But beware of people whose smile doesn't
extend to their eyes.

NOTES

TAKE
YOUR
TIME

You don't have to "work the room". Some
people need to speak to everyone in the
room before the session ends. Don't
become "that guy". Give each person you
meet as much time as they deserve.

NOTES

STAND
NEXT TO
THE FOOD

Everyone will come to you eventually.

NOTES

STAND BY THE
REGISTRATION
DESK AND
GREET
EVERYONE
THAT COMES IN

There's no faster way to meet everyone.
Later, you can focus on individuals.

NOTES

FIND

AN

OPEN GROUP

OF 2 – 3 PEOPLE AND

JOIN IN

Turn this page to discover an easy way to spot an open group.

THE POCKET GUIDE FOR
NERVOUS NETWORKERS

NOTES

HOW TO
SPOT AN
OPEN GROUP
OF 3 OR MORE
PEOPLE?

From above the group looks like the letter C.

NOTES

HOW TO SPOT
A
CLOSED
GROUP?

From above, they'll look like the number
ZERO. Because that's how many people
they'll welcome into their conversation.
Avoid this kind of group. These people are
not here to network.

NOTES

PAUSE

AFTER YOU

ENTER

THE

ROOM

Look around. Take your time to see who's
there and decide who you want to connect
with, before you begin.

NOTES

EAT BEFORE
YOU
GET THERE

That way you won't have to juggle food and drink when you need to reach for your business card. You're not there for the food.

NOTES

DRESS
APPROPRIATELY
FOR
THE EVENT

Try to match the occasion. Sometimes it's a suit, sometimes it's not. If in doubt though, dress more formally than you want. It's better to be over-dressed than under-dressed.

NOTES

LOOK
SMART

...but make sure your clothes are comfortable. Don't forget details like hair, nails, shoes (a speaker I know destroyed his credibility with the audience by wearing scuffed shoes during a speech about the importance of appearance).

NOTES

DON'T
BE A
FASHION VICTIM
BUT DON'T LOOK

OUT
OF
DATE
EITHER

If your words say 21st Century but your clothes say 1980, you'll lose your credibility and with it, the trust of the people you're talking to. If in doubt, go for elegant classics, they're timeless.

NOTES

SHUT UP
AND
LISTEN

My parents taught me to talk only when I
have value to add to the conversation. This
advice has made me more valuable
connections over the years than I can count.

NOTES

LISTEN
CLOSELY

Business is basically helping people in exchange for money. The person you're talking with will tell you everything you need to know in order to help them. Just ask them the right questions and pay attention.

NOTES

MAKE

NOTES

A good place to do this is often on the reverse of their business card, so you can follow up. Don't rely on your memory, that never works. Some networkers carry a notepad with them (the Notes app on your phone works too).

If you want to make sure you don't miss a golden opportunity, you could even take a photo of their card with your phone and email it to yourself with notes about your conversation with that person.

NOTES

DON'T

GET

DRUNK.

REALLY. IT HAPPENS.

Don't be that guy. Even at 'party' networking events. Your reputation takes longer to recover than your head does.

NOTES

THOU SHALT NOT SELL

Don't try to sell at networking events. Meet people who may need your product or service, but arrange to meet them later in a follow-up meeting.

NOTES

DON'T HIDE
AMONGST
YOUR
FRIENDS

You're there to make new ones.

NOTES

BEFORE YOU OPEN YOUR MOUTH THINK: WHAT'S IN IT FOR THEM?

NOTES

HELP
OTHER PEOPLE
MAKE
USEFUL
CONNECTIONS

Useful to them. Do this often and you'll
become known as a person who brings
value to every meeting.

NOTES

OFFER
YOUR CARD
ONLY IF
THEY OFFER
THEIRS
OR ASK FOR YOURS

If you want to connect and they don't offer first, it's okay to ask for their card, but don't offer yours unless asked for it because they may not want yours. Don't cast your business cards around like confetti.

NOTES

SHOW
RESPECT

When they hand you their business card, take a second to look at it before putting it away. Trust me, they'll notice.

There's a lot more I could say about the power of showing respect. Maybe in the next book…

NOTES

CONVERSATION
STARTERS

NOTES

HELLO,
MY NAME IS _____,
WHAT'S YOURS?

It may seem basic, but you'd be amazed at
how many people I see forget to use this
simple introduction.

NOTES

I LOVE
HEARING ABOUT WHAT
PEOPLE
DO
FOR A LIVING.
WHAT DO
YOU
DO?

CONVERSATION STARTERS

NOTES

HOW
CAN I HELP
YOU
FIND
MORE
CLIENTS?

Who isn't looking for more clients?

NOTES

WHO ARE
YOUR BUSINESS
HEROES
OR
HEROINES?

You can tell a lot about a person by
discovering their role models. This can be a
good starting point for a conversation about
why they do what they do and their
inspiration. That could lead anywhere.

THE POCKET GUIDE FOR
NERVOUS NETWORKERS

NOTES

WHY

DID YOU

START

YOUR OWN

BUSINESS?

Find out more about them before you start talking about yourself. It can give you important clues as to how you could help them out.

NOTES

WHAT IS
YOUR
IDEAL CLIENT?
PERHAPS
I KNOW
ONE OR TWO.

If you can use your network to help others,
they'll remember it and may even look for
ways to return the favour. Some experts call
this the "Law of Reciprocity".

CONVERSATION STARTERS

THE POCKET GUIDE FOR NERVOUS NETWORKERS

NOTES

I LOVE HELPING
PEOPLE CONNECT
WITH PEOPLE IN
MY NETWORK.
TO WHAT KIND OF
PEOPLE
OR
BUSINESSES
WOULD
YOU
LIKE TO BE
INTRODUCED?

NOTES

HOW HAS
(A RECENT EVENT)
AFFECTED
YOUR
BUSINESS?

Try to pick a positive event (such as a recent sporting victory or local public celebration) but if you really can't think of one, use whatever you can (maybe flooding or construction work has been affecting access to local businesses).

NOTES

WHAT
INSPIRED YOU
TO COME TO
THIS EVENT
TODAY?

This can produce surprisingly useful information.

I find this is often a way to find out their 'pain or pleasure points'. Maybe they're a new business and need to raise their profile, so you could introduce them to PR specialists or a friendly journalist.

NOTES

WHAT
DO
YOU ENJOY
MOST ABOUT THE
WORK
THAT YOU DO?

This can give you valuable clues as to their motivations and expectations. You can take their response in a number of directions to continue the conversation.

NOTES

HOW LONG
HAVE YOU
WORKED
FOR
XYZ CORP?

Obviously, don't use this on someone who
has just started a new business!

CONVERSATION STARTERS

THE POCKET GUIDE FOR NERVOUS NETWORKERS

NOTES

WHY
DID YOU DECIDE
TO JOIN
XYZ CORP?

CONVERSATION STARTERS

NOTES

ASK
WHERE THEIR
BUSINESS
OR
INDUSTRY
IS
GOING
IN THE
NEXT 3 YEARS

Everyone loves to be asked for their opinion.
Listen closely to their answers so you can
ask follow-up questions.

CONVERSATION STARTERS

THE POCKET GUIDE FOR NERVOUS NETWORKERS

NOTES

ARE YOU A
REGULAR
AT THESE
EVENTS?

This is the business equivalent of "Do you
come here often?" which may be a cliché,
but it works pretty well. If they are new,
follow up with "Let me introduce you to
some people" or "What convinced you to
visit today?"

NOTES

WHERE
HAVE YOU
TRAVELLED
FROM
TODAY?

There's a follow-up question on the next
page. It's always a good idea to have two
questions in case the first one falls flat.

CONVERSATION STARTERS

THE POCKET GUIDE FOR NERVOUS NETWORKERS

NOTES

WHAT
WOULD YOU
MOST
LIKE TO
IMPROVE
FOR YOUR
CLIENTS?

NOTES

LISTEN

FOR

CLUES

Such as recent holidays, films they have seen, pastimes etc. Sometimes the best conversational openings come from just listening to the things your group are saying to one another.

NOTES

LISTEN
FOR
ANYTHING
YOU MAY HAVE
IN COMMON

Family, regional accent and sporting
interests are all great clues.

NOTES

LOOK
FOR
MORE CLUES

Such as club ties or pins. You could also ask what they're reading currently. Lead into it by mentioning something you've read.

NOTES

WEAR

A DISTINCTIVE

CLUE

OF YOUR OWN

Help them out by wearing something yourself that can trigger a conversation. Don't dress like a clown though. Unless you're a fancy dress outfitter, in which case you should definitely dress like a clown "I may look like a clown but I'm all business when it comes to customer service…"

NOTES

NEVER
GIVE
ONE WORD
ANSWERS

I've often wondered why people do this at networking events. Why go there if you don't want to have conversations? If it's because you're shy or introverted, rehearse your conversational skills before you go out networking.

NOTES

AVOID
CONSTANT
FLIPPANCY

Or you run the risk of being written off as a
business lightweight.

NOTES

ASK
OPEN
QUESTIONS

CONVERSATION STARTERS

Because they invite detailed answers and that invites conversation.

Open questions are ones that don't have a "yes" or "no" answer. For example, instead of "Are you a lawyer?" try: "What motivated you to become a lawyer?"

THE POCKET GUIDE FOR NERVOUS NETWORKERS

NOTES

AVOID
DISCUSSING
POLITICS
OR
RELIGION

Really, people do and it rarely works out well
at a networking event. Keep to safe topics.

CONVERSATION STARTERS

THE POCKET GUIDE FOR NERVOUS NETWORKERS

**THE POCKET GUIDE FOR
NERVOUS NETWORKERS**

NOTES

THIS IS
A
NO WHINE
ZONE

Keep the tone of your conversation positive.
Nobody likes a whiner.

NOTES

END
CONVERSATIONS
GRACEFULLY

Don't get trapped in the corner by one person. After you've chatted, introduce them to someone useful to them, and then move away. Just walking away is rude.

NOTES

FOLLOWING UP

NOTES

WITHIN 24hrs SUGGEST

MEETING

FOR A

COFFEE

AND

CHAT

Trust me, this doesn't have to be a sales
pitch. There's plenty of time for that.

NOTES

SUGGEST
YOU MEET FOR
10 MINUTES
ON A DAY OF
THEIR CHOICE

Who can't spare ten minutes? Never go over
that ten minutes though. Leave them
wanting more.

NOTES

HOLD
FOLLOW UP
MEETINGS
AWAY
FROM
THEIR OFFICE

This way they won't get distracted by customers or colleagues. If they're not prepared to do that, they probably don't really want to meet you. Move on to the next person.

NOTES

SEND THEM
USEFUL AND RELEVANT
LINKS
VIA
SOCIAL
MEDIA

This means actually useful things. Funny cat videos don't count.

NOTES

SEND THEM
USEFUL AND RELEVANT
LINKS
VIA
EMAIL

Once again, keep it useful to them. A list of
your product's features does not come
under this category.

NOTES

SEND
A
CONNECTION
REQUEST VIA THEIR
FAVOURITE
SOCIAL MEDIA
PLATFORMS

Stick to just the main one or two.

Nobody joins new platforms just to connect with one person.

NOTES

FOLLOW UP
WITHIN
24 HOURS

There is an expiration date on connecting
with people who you've only just met.

THE POCKET GUIDE FOR
NERVOUS NETWORKERS

NOTES

BE
PATIENT

Building valuable relationships takes time.

NOTES

FIND A WAY
OF
CONNECTING
THE
PEOPLE YOU MEET
TO
POTENTIAL LEADS

Think like a business match-maker. They'll both love you for it and want to pay the favour back. There's a very strong human urge to repay a favour soon after it's given.

NOTES

WHY DO WE NETWORK?

A BONUS ARTICLE TO HELP YOU ALONG THE ROAD TO NETWORKING SUCCESS

NOTES

WHY DO WE NETWORK?

We humans are a funny lot.

From the moment we're born, we see other people interacting and pretty quickly, we realise that we want a piece of that action.

It looks great: people laughing with each other and sharing food, toys, and information with each other.

As we get older, we realise that some of that information is hidden. Like where the sweets are kept in the kitchen. Or an older sibling might let on that there are secrets to getting on with the opposite sex.

Where would we be if we didn't have access to that secret information?

FRIENDS WITH BENEFITS

It doesn't take long for us to realise that there are many benefits to being friends with people. This is as true in business as in every other aspect of life.

Business friends can let you know when opportunities arise. Business friends can tell you who it is good to work with as well as who to avoid, and if you think that isn't worth knowing, you probably haven't been in business for long. Knowing who to rely on and who is just looking out for themselves can mean the difference between achieving success or filing for bankruptcy.

THE 3 TRUTHS OF NETWORKING

Successful business networking is not as dark and mysterious as some people would have you believe. Here are three truths you need to know before you begin:

- If you think business networking is about going to an event and trying to sell something to someone there, you can get that idea out of your head right now.

- If you think business networking is about being grilled by strangers for an hour and then discarded, forget that notion.

- If you think business networking is going to solve all your problems, you can forget that idea too.

Successful business networking is about finding people who you like and make sense when you talk to them. It's about locating people who you get along with and who you may even be able to learn from. People who you might like to talk to again.

In other words, people with whom you might actually become friends.

The fact is that we would all much rather do business with friends than strangers. Why wouldn't we?

So your task when networking is to make some friends.

Here's something else that will surprise you: these people may never buy from you.

What?! Shock! Horror!

The point is that every person you meet has a network of business connections that they are friendly with. A network that trusts their judgement and recommendations. And some of *those* people may be interested in buying what you offer.

TRUST MARKETING

It doesn't matter if your business offers a service or a product, we are all in the business of using "trust marketing". If a potential client does not trust you or your product, they will walk away. If they trust you, they are much more inclined to trust your product or service. Price is only one tiny factor; far more important is whether they trust you.

It is that simple. When it comes to networking, you need to make friends, and if they believe in your quality they will be much more inclined to recommend you to the people in their network that trust their judgement.

THE 3 STEPS OF NETWORKING

The first step of all networking is about making a connection. Networking events are designed to enable this to happen, but throwing people together is not enough. Meeting people and getting on with them is not always simple; this book was written to help you with that.

The second step is to find a way to give value to that connection so that the other person wants to keep coming back to you. We are all experts in our own area of activity. For example, I could never hope to do my own tax returns, but if you can share some tips on making it easier for me, I might well seek you out again or connect you with someone I know that could use your help.

The third step comes when they recognise your value and want to reciprocate. There is a term that some behaviourists call the Law of Reciprocity. It boils down to this: if you do me a favour I feel a very strong urge to do one for you. This is the basis of a lot of those "free offer" deals that retailers or direct mail marketers try to make. They believe that if they send you a free pen, you are more inclined to sign up to their travel insurance plan. It doesn't always work, but it works often enough for them to keep doing it.

It also works on a much less cynical basis between friends. If you are a source of good advice, professional guidance, or even just a sensible level-headed sounding board for their ideas, it adds to the amount of trust your business friends (also called your personal network) have in you.

The more help you give them, the more they want to help you. If that means letting you know when they hear about a new business opportunity, or recommending you to someone else in their personal network, all the better.

So, to recap:

1. **Make friends** (use the tips in this guide).

2. **Give value.**

3. **Be there when they want to reciprocate.**

Then do it all over again.

NOTES

NOTES